M000073435

you are the way

DEVOTIONS FOR LENT 2018

AUGSBURG FORTRESS

Minneapolis

YOU ARE THE WAY
Devotions for Lent 2018

Scripture quotations are from the New Revised Standard Version Bible, copyright © 1989 by the Division of Christian Education of the National Council of the Churches of Christ in the USA. Used by permission. All rights reserved.

References to ELW are from *Evangelical Lutheran Worship*, copyright © 2006 Evangelical Lutheran Church in America.

ISBN 978-1-5064-3151-2

Writers: Kevin Ruffcorn (February 14–24), Harvard Stephens Jr. (February 25–March 3), Karoline Lewis (March 4–17), Jennifer Baker-Trinity (March 18–31)
Editors: Suzanne Burke, Laurie J. Hanson
Cover image: Tamie Steffen-Hornstein, www.tamiehornstein.com
Cover design: Laurie Ingram
Interior design: Eileen Engebretson
Typesetting: Lauren Williamson

The paper used in this publication meets the minimum requirements of American National Standard for Information Sciences—Permanence of Paper for Printed Library Materials, ANSI Z329.48-1984.

Manufactured in the U.S.A.

18 17   1 2 3 4 5 6 7 8 9 10

Welcome

In the Gospel of John, Jesus describes himself with a series of "I am" statements. Most of these include an image (light of the world, good shepherd, and so on). *You Are the Way* explores one or more "I am" sayings of Jesus during each week in Lent:

+ "I am the way, and the truth, and the life" (February 14–17)
+ "I am the gate"; "I am the good shepherd" (February 18–24)
+ "I am the light of the world" (February 25–March 3)
+ "I am the true vine"; "I am the vine, you are the branches" (March 4–10)
+ "I AM" (March 11–17)
+ "I am the bread of life"; "I am the living bread that came down from heaven" (March 18–24)
+ "I am the resurrection and the life" (March 25–31)

Each of these devotions offers an evocative image, a reading from John, a quotation to ponder, a reflection, and a prayer. The writers bring their unique voices and pastoral wisdom to reflect on the gospel texts. Some of these texts will be read in worship during this liturgical year (year B of the Revised Common Lectionary).

May you follow Jesus, who is the way, through the days of Lent to the empty tomb.

—The editors

February 14 / Ash Wednesday

John 14:1-4

[Jesus said to his disciples,] "Do not let your hearts be troubled. Believe in God, believe also in me. In my Father's house there are many dwelling places. If it were not so, would I have told you that I go to prepare a place for you? And if I go and prepare a place for you, I will come again and will take you to myself, so that where I am, there you may be also. And you know the way to the place where I am going."

To ponder

Only until all human beings begin to recognize themselves as human beings will prejudice be gone forever. People ask me what race I am . . . I just answer: "I'm a member of the human race."
— Amelia Boynton Robinson, *Bridge across Jordan*

4

A place for you

Clarence stood across the street and surveyed the building that was once a restaurant. Now the windows were boarded up, the doors padlocked, the paint peeling. Fifty years ago it had been a bustling enterprise. As he looked, Clarence remembered an incident that was seared into his mind. He and his family had tried to eat at that restaurant and were told there was no room for people like them. The shame and anger he felt then became real once again.

Jesus' disciples were a ragtag band of men. Among them were rough, earthy fishermen, a despised tax collector, and a political zealot of whom many were suspicious. They did not see themselves as holy like the Pharisees, or righteous. Jesus' words, "I go and prepare a place for you," were words of comfort and strength. They were included.

As we receive the ashes on our brows, we remember that there is room for everyone at the foot of Jesus' cross. We acknowledge that heaven is not a gated community and no one need be excluded. Living in God's kingdom today, we strive to experience the equality and unity it brings.

Prayer

Sovereign Lord, today as we acknowledge our common sinfulness, empower us also to live in the truth that all are your children and people whom you love. Amen.

February 15

John 14:5-7

Thomas said to [Jesus], "Lord, we do not know where you are going. How can we know the way?" Jesus said to him, "I am the way, and the truth, and the life. No one comes to the Father except through me. If you know me, you will know my Father also. From now on you do know him and have seen him."

To ponder

Two roads diverged in a yellow wood, / And sorry I could not travel both . . . I shall be telling this with a sigh / Somewhere ages and ages hence: / Two roads diverged in a wood, and I— / I took the one less traveled by, / And that has made all the difference.
—Robert Frost, "The Road Not Taken"

The way of Jesus

After searching thirty minutes and not finding the business location, Carlota admitted she was lost. She drove into a gas station and asked for directions. An older man behind the counter described the turns Carlota needed to take, which she dutifully wrote down. After another twenty minutes, Carlota realized she was still lost. Pulling over to the curb, Carlota asked a young student if she knew where the business was. "Oh sure, it's just a couple blocks away," the girl replied. "If you want, I'll show you the way." Jumping into Carlota's car, the girl guided her and within minutes Carlota arrived at her destination.

Early Christians identified themselves as followers of "the Way." Applying the teachings of Jesus to their lives, the early Christians loved the people around them. They supported widows and orphans, cared for the sick and dying, accepted people who had been ostracized, and welcomed those who were marginalized into their fellowship. Guided and empowered by the Holy Spirit, these followers of the Way transformed the world. As followers of the Way, we carry on their ministry.

Prayer

Guide us, Jesus, along the paths of our lives. If we wander or get lost, bring us back to the path. While we walk, enable us to boldly and lovingly invite others to join us on the journey. Amen.

John 14:8-10

Philip said to [Jesus], "Lord, show us the Father, and we will be satisfied." Jesus said to him, "Have I been with you all this time, Philip, and you still do not know me? Whoever has seen me has seen the Father. How can you say, 'Show us the Father'? Do you not believe that I am in the Father and the Father is in me? The words that I say to you I do not speak on my own; but the Father who dwells in me does his works."

To ponder

People who live together naturally catch the looks and air of one another and without having one feature alike, they contract a some-thing in the whole countenance which strikes one as a resemblance.
—Frances Burney, *The Early Journals and Letters of Fanny Burney*

A family resemblance

The extended family of Michael Diego Kelly Lopez crowded into the hospital room. They were there to welcome him into their family. He was wrapped in a blanket and perched in his mother's arms, only his face peeking out of the folds. Everyone agreed that "Mickey Dee" had his mother's eyes and his father's strong forehead. "Look, he's got Tio Juan's nose," piped up a voice. "Yeah, and that's an O'Malley chin if I've ever seen one," added another. It was obvious to everyone that the child belonged in the family.

Jesus was the spitting image of God. Philip didn't recognize the resemblance, but it was there. Jesus' love for people who were poor, ignored, and marginalized reflected the Father's values. Jesus' longing to make broken people whole was an extension of God's desire. In becoming one of us, and experiencing life with all of creation, Jesus demonstrated the importance God places on relationships.

We are members of God's family. The Holy Spirit moves within us to reflect this reality. We may not be spitting images, but we pray that when people see us, they catch a glimpse of what God is like.

Prayer

Move within us, Holy Spirit, so that our words and actions are proclamations of your gospel and demonstrations of your love. Amen.

John 14:11-13

[Jesus said,] "Believe me that I am in the Father and the Father is in me; but if you do not, then believe me because of the works themselves. Very truly, I tell you, the one who believes in me will also do the works that I do and, in fact, will do greater works than these, because I am going to the Father. I will do whatever you ask in my name, so that the Father may be glorified in the Son."

To ponder

We know only too well that what we are doing is nothing more than a drop in the ocean. But if the drop were not there, the ocean would be missing something.

—Mother Teresa, *Stories Told by Mother Teresa*

God at work

Jesus is in God and God is in Jesus. This is heady stuff, almost impossible to conceptualize and difficult to explain. Part of what it means is that Jesus does things only God can do. Stilling a storm and feeding five thousand people with two fish and five loaves of bread were acts of God. Cleansing lepers, dining with sinners, and forgiving people's sin demonstrated the depth of God's love. Jesus raised the dead and, in God's greatest act, was himself raised from the dead. In Jesus we see God moving in the world. Our response is to believe.

God's activity didn't end with Jesus. The Holy Spirit moves through God's people to house people who are homeless, feed those who hunger, and build hospitals that bring healing to people who are sick or injured. Today we are privileged to be a part of God's work in our world.

Prayer

Lord, may our hands do your work, our mouths proclaim your word, and our hearts share your love. Amen.

February 18 / Lent 1

John 10:1-3

[Jesus said,] "Very truly, I tell you, anyone who does not enter the sheepfold by the gate but climbs in by another way is a thief and a bandit. The one who enters by the gate is the shepherd of the sheep. The gatekeeper opens the gate for him, and the sheep hear his voice. He calls his own sheep by name and leads them out."

To ponder

We've got this gift of love, but love is like a precious plant. You can't just accept it and leave it in the cupboard or just think it's going to get on by itself. You've got to keep watering it. You've got to really look after it and nurture it.
—John Lennon, "Man of the Decade" interview

A strong bond

Sheep are timid animals, easily frightened by strangers. Though they don't mind being alone, they crave significant relationships. They have this kind of relationship with their shepherd. The shepherd brings them to green pastures, leads them beside still waters, and keeps them safe. This care and protection forms a strong bond with the sheep, a bond that enables them to truly rest in the shepherd's presence.

We too long for deep, lasting relationships. We want someone to notice us and to accept us for who we are—warts and all—yet encourage us to be more than we are. We hunger after relationships that are safe, where we can be comfortable and let down our guard. Relationships with those who stick by us through thick and thin are precious to us.

Our shepherd, Jesus, has such a relationship with us. While we celebrate this relationship, we also reach out to others who are looking for love and acceptance.

Prayer

Thank you, Lord, for your presence with us. May it give us both rest and the motivation to act. Amen.

February 19

John 10:4-6

"When he has brought out all his own, he goes ahead of them, and the sheep follow him because they know his voice. They will not follow a stranger, but they will run from him because they do not know the voice of strangers." Jesus used this figure of speech with them, but they did not understand what he was saying to them.

To ponder

He ne'er is crowned with immortality / Who fears to follow where airy voices lead.
—John Keats, *The Complete Poetical Works and Letters of John Keats*

Listening for God's voice

It happened in a split second. Kenyon and his father were in the stadium, on the way to the men's room. One moment Kenyon was holding on to his father's hand, and the next he was alone in a crowd of strangers. A tsunami of panic surged over Kenyon. All he could see were legs as the throng pushed and bumped him. "Dad!" he screamed, but his voice was drowned out by the noise of the crowd. Then, above the din, Kenyon heard a sound that calmed his fears. He heard his father's voice yelling, "Kenyon!" It was faint and distant. Kenyon headed toward the voice. The voice guided his steps and grew louder. The crowd thinned and Kenyon saw his father. He yelled. His father turned. Seeing each other, they flew into each other's arms.

Though we may have difficulty hearing God's voice, God speaks to us in many ways. We may hear God's voice while reading scripture, remembering the promise of baptism, or sharing bread and wine. At times, we may hear God speak through the words of friends, the advice of a mentor, or a time of prayer. In whatever ways God speaks, the voice of our shepherd comforts us and leads us.

Prayer

Lord, speak to us, that we may speak in living echoes of your tone. Amen. (ELW 676)

John 10:7-8

So again Jesus said to them, "Very truly, I tell you, I am the gate for the sheep. All who came before me are thieves and bandits; but the sheep did not listen to them."

To ponder

If you spend time judging and criticizing people, you will not have time to heal from your pain or brokenness. You cannot love yourself when you judge or criticize others who are created in God's image and after His Likeness . . . in which you are also created. Love cannot operate from a space of pain. Love and hurt cannot reside in the same space.

—Kemi Sogunle, *Beyond the Pain*

The gate to forgiveness

When we are worshiping and sharing fellowship in a Christian community, it doesn't take long before we are hurt. The church is part of God's kingdom, but also a very human institution. Someone in the congregation may make a derogatory comment about a family member. The pastor may use a sermon illustration that seems to oppose our political position. We may not receive a thank-you for our hard work, or we find ourselves a subject in the rumor mill. Yes, we all have been the victims of thieves and bandits.

To continue to live in community, we need to give and receive forgiveness. This is possible because of the forgiveness we have already received through Christ. We put away our fears of being hurt again and step through the gate—Jesus. When we walk into the future, we do so with confidence. Jesus has promised to be with us always (Matthew 28:20). We are also assured that nothing in all creation "will be able to separate us from the love of God in Christ Jesus our Lord" (Romans 8:39).

Prayer

Lord, we know the power of our words and actions to hurt and to heal. Grant us the ability to forgive those who have hurt us, and to ask for forgiveness from those we have hurt. Anoint our words and actions that they may heal. Amen.

February 21

John 10:9-10

[Jesus said,] "I am the gate. Whoever enters by me will be saved, and will come in and go out and find pasture. The thief comes only to steal and kill and destroy. I came that they may have life, and have it abundantly."

To ponder

It is a fatal mistake to assume that God's goal for your life is material prosperity or popular success, as the world defines it. The abundant life has nothing to do with material abundance, and faithfulness to God does not guarantee success in a career or even ministry. Never focus on temporary crowns.

—Rick Warren, "Remember: You're Not Home Yet"

Don't settle for the good life

Everyone chases their own idea of "the good life." A businesswoman strives for a seven-figure income and an executive suite on the 42nd floor. An immigrant family enters this country seeking a new life and an opportunity to have a hopeful future. A young couple struggles to pay off college loans and reach a point where money coming in is greater than money going out. People who are chronically ill long for a breath that comes easy, an end to treatments, or movement without pain.

These are all notable achievements and wonderful gifts, but they are not the definition of the abundant life that Jesus came to give us. Jesus' gift of abundant life is available to all, no matter your economic status, physical location, or health. Jesus came that we might see God's love and live in a dynamic relationship with God. The abundant life gives us purpose beyond ourselves and the opportunity to use our talents to serve others and touch their lives with God's grace. Jesus calls his followers not to settle for the good life, but to experience the abundant life.

Prayer

For the well-being of ourselves and those around us, Lord, prevent us from living anything less than your abundant life. Amen.

February 22

John 10:11-13

[Jesus said,] "I am the good shepherd. The good shepherd lays down his life for the sheep. The hired hand, who is not the shepherd and does not own the sheep, sees the wolf coming and leaves the sheep and runs away—and the wolf snatches them and scatters them. The hired hand runs away because a hired hand does not care for the sheep."

To ponder

Love will find a way through paths where wolves fear to prey.
—Lord Byron, *Lord Byron Complete Works Ultimate Collection*

In the shepherd's care

Wolves are often portrayed as frightening, dangerous creatures. We have the wolf that tried to eat Little Red Riding Hood, and another wolf that tried to blow down the homes of the three little pigs. When danger lurks we say, "A wolf stands at our door," and during a full moon there's always the "threat" of encountering a werewolf (a man/wolf).

Wolves hunt in packs. If a pack of wolves attacked a flock of sheep, we can understand why hired hands would run away. Hired hands aren't paid enough to lose their lives over a little wool and a couple of pounds of meat.

Jesus, the good shepherd, doesn't leave his flock defenseless. He surrounds us and shields us with his love. His presence and power provide us with peace, courage, and hope in the face of danger. Our shepherd has even died for us, so we no longer need to fear the Death Wolf. Following Jesus, we can safely and boldly go places where even wolves fear to tread.

Prayer

Savior like a shepherd lead us; much we need your tender care . . . . We are yours; in love befriend us, be the guardian of our way. Amen. (ELW 789, stanzas 1 and 2)

John 10:14-16

[Jesus said,] "I am the good shepherd. I know my own and my own know me, just as the Father knows me and I know the Father. And I lay down my life for the sheep. I have other sheep that do not belong to this fold. I must bring them also, and they will listen to my voice. So there will be one flock, one shepherd."

To ponder

I do verily believe that when God shall accomplish [unity], it will be the effect of love, and not the cause of love. It will proceed from love, before it brings forth love.

—John Owen, in *The Golden Treasury of Puritan Quotations*

Unity

Emily Ann's parents carefully explained to her that her new brother was in Mommy's tummy. In a few months, the baby would be born and Emily Ann would become an older sister. Emily Ann was excited. In the days that followed she frequently talked about her new brother. She pretended that her doll was her new brother and practiced caring for him.

Everything went well until Emily Ann's parents brought her new baby brother home from the hospital. She could hardly wait to hold Timothy John. Quickly, though, Emily Ann began to realize that Mommy and Daddy were spending a lot of time with Timothy John. They would walk around patting him on his back, or rock him in the same chair in which they used to rock her. Emily Ann became envious of all the time her parents were spending with Timothy John. She started acting out to get their attention. Emily Ann's family didn't really become a family until her parents assured her that they loved her as much as they ever did.

We don't know who the other sheep in the shepherd's flock will be, but we do know that God has enough love to love us all.

Prayer

Lord, help us to welcome others and celebrate our unity in you. Amen.

John 10:17-18

[Jesus said,] "For this reason the Father loves me, because I lay down my life in order to take it up again. No one takes it from me, but I lay it down of my own accord. I have power to lay it down, and I have power to take it up again. I have received this command from my Father."

To ponder

I have been astonished that men could die martyrs / for their religion— / I have shuddered at it, / I shudder no more. / I could be martyred for my religion. Love is my religion / and I could die for that. I could die for you. / My Creed is Love and you are its only tenet.

—John Keats, *The Complete Poetical Works and Letters of John Keats*

24

So that we might live

Jesus stood before the Jewish authorities as they gathered to pass judgment on him. They congratulated themselves on trapping Jesus. Betrayed by one of his own disciples, Jesus was captured by the temple guard late at night, when his followers wouldn't be there to oppose them. They convicted him that night of blasphemy. In the morning they sent him to Pilate and accused Jesus of treason. The authorities had salted the crowd with their people, who started to chant, "Crucify him!"

The religious authorities thought they had trapped Jesus, but they hadn't. In obedience to his Father's will, Jesus laid down his life for all humankind. He allowed the Roman soldiers to lead him to Golgotha and to nail him to the wooden beam of a cross, on which he would give up his life.

Jesus did all this out of divine love. His actions opened us up to God's grace and restored our relationship with God. His life and death demonstrated to us the true meaning and purpose of life. We will never be the same because of what Jesus accomplished.

Prayer

Thank you, Lord, that you willingly laid down your life so that we might live. Amen.

February 25 / Lent 2

John 8:12

Again Jesus spoke to them, saying, "I am the light of the world. Whoever follows me will never walk in darkness but will have the light of life."

To ponder

This may be stating the obvious, but we do see what we want to see. What we call "seeing" is generally a reflection of our inner dialogue, which is constant and unceasing. . . . We have our own agendas, our predisposed attitudes, and our own cultural biases. We rarely see the world in a fresh way. . . . Seeing can be cultivated, indeed must be, if we wish to live full and productive lives, sensitively receiving and richly giving to ourselves and others. . . .

Learning to see, learning to be, and learning to come into accord with the deeper sources within and without—these are undoubtedly the greatest challenges given us, the most potent tests of our creative aspirations and capabilities.
—David Ulrich, "Awakening Sight"

To see more clearly

The light of Jesus appears as our faith comes alive, sometimes in surprising ways. Jesus is the light of the world, and sometimes we too are called the light of the world. As we follow Jesus, this light can be shared. If we allow ourselves time and space to slow down a bit, listen, and appreciate the light of Christ in other people and in the wonders of creation, we may perceive more clearly (and not through eyes alone) how that same light enfolds us—as individuals and as a community in Christ.

Today we celebrate the power of God's presence in our world and in our lives as we encounter words that are simple and yet profoundly mysterious. Jesus says, *I am light—for the whole world; follow me; you'll never walk in darkness.*

Prayer

Mysterious One, we pray in celebration of your magnificent light. Thank you for all the ways you offer this gift—to us, through us, and in the wonders of your creation. Take away our fear of darkness, because the light you give brings us peace and security, even when darkness is all we can see. Amen.

February 26

John 8:13-14

Then the Pharisees said to him, "You are testifying on your own behalf; your testimony is not valid." Jesus answered, "Even if I testify on my own behalf, my testimony is valid because I know where I have come from and where I am going, but you do not know where I come from or where I am going."

To ponder

"You can only get your heart broke so many times before you forget how to offer it up at all. I don't want that to happen to my boy" ... There was something sweet about being asked so formally not to break somebody's heart.

—Pearl Cleage, *Some Things I Never Thought I'd Do*

Show us the way

Jesus is the way, and where he leads us will surely surprise us. He knows the paths we have yet to discover. He leads us beyond the boundaries of places that are familiar and comfortable to us. His light reveals possibilities we have never imagined. His grace and forgiveness defend us from the cruel judgments of others. His vision for our lives is wonderfully liberating. He shows us deeper truths about our own potential. How wonderful it is to know his presence, hear his voice, receive his power. This is how we begin to realize what we are meant to be. This is how our destiny as children of God unfolds.

These gracious gifts are not merely for our own fulfillment. Never forget that we are called to participate in God's great mission to make this world whole. For the faithful in Christ, the holy scriptures become God's sweet request: *Heal hearts, don't break them; this is how you walk in my light.*

Prayer

Giver of light, we ask you today for a new sense of direction. Show us where you want us to go. Teach us how to walk with others in peace. Fill our hearts with your wisdom and courage so that we find our place beside you. Amen.

John 8:18-20

[Jesus said,] "I testify on my own behalf, and the Father who sent me testifies on my behalf." Then [the Pharisees] said to him, "Where is your Father?" Jesus answered, "You know neither me nor my Father. If you knew me, you would know my Father also." He spoke these words while he was teaching in the treasury of the temple, but no one arrested him, because his hour had not yet come.

To ponder

If going to the theater or movies was to be shown life at its worst, then dancing was to be a participant in that same type of degraded existence, a forum for excited passions and surrounded by a culture that promoted liquor and easy virtue. . . . A similar sort

of attack was often launched against all sorts of popular amuse-
ments, from card playing and gambling to popular jazz music and
the instrument of its transmission—the radio.
—Maria Erling and Mark Granquist, *The Augustana Story*

Light in a changing world

People are often unprepared for the cultural and scientific innovations that impact their lives. Today we deal with remarkable
technological innovations and unprecedented multicultural inter-
actions—enhanced and amplified by many forms of social media.

Jesus himself is a remarkable innovator, and his relationship
with God the Father is groundbreaking in every way. He celebrates a world that most of his contemporaries can barely fathom.

Trust that Christ is present as we are challenged by difficult
racial and interfaith encounters, broadening expressions of gender
identity, an increasingly fragile ecological system, and a widening
gap between the rich and the poor. Trust the Holy Spirit as we as
engage in dialogue and discernment supported by patience and
humility. This changing world needs to hear the testimonies we
offer in Jesus' name.

Prayer

Great teacher, you have promised to fill us with your light. Teach
us patience. Give us courage. Increase our ability to recognize
your presence among us. Show us how to bring tradition and
innovation together to honor you and serve you in today's world.
Amen.

John 9:1-4

As [Jesus] walked along, he saw a man blind from birth. His disciples asked him, "Rabbi, who sinned, this man or his parents, that he was born blind?" Jesus answered, "Neither this man nor his parents sinned; he was born blind so that God's works might be revealed in him. We must work the works of him who sent me while it is day; night is coming when no one can work."

To ponder

Everybody who loved me wanted me to be innocent—tricked, duped, all unawares. But of course, that was not the case. All those years ago I wanted to have an adventure, an outrageous experience, and the fact of it being illegal made it all the more exciting. . . . I had long ago accepted that I had to pay consequences.

32

I am capable of making terrible mistakes, and I am also prepared to take responsibility for my actions.

—Piper Kerman, *Orange Is the New Black: My Year in a Woman's Prison*

Seeing possibilities

Day and night, black and white: why do we so readily believe that the things of this world are either one or the other? When an incarcerated woman reflects on her past, her crimes, and the meaning of justice and redemption, we do well to pay attention. She may help us to see why the blame game makes things too simple, predictable, and ultimately unfair.

Jesus knows the complexities of life, and he discerns the possibilities that lie beyond our inclinations to reduce our lives to superficial calculations of cause and effect. Who sinned? We all do, but Jesus' light reveals the power of grace—and its divine intrusion into our systems of blame and punishment. For Jesus, the day represents all the possibilities of God's power to heal and restore us. Beyond black and white, there is room for all people, all colors, and all stories that show the power of God working in our lives. What color is your story today?

Prayer

Great redeemer, we pray today for patience and openness to the power of your love. Remind us to love ourselves as well as others. Keep us from letting blame overshadow the light of your gracious presence in our lives. Help us to believe again that all things are possible when we are in your loving embrace. Amen.

March 1

John 9:5-7

"As long as I am in the world, I am the light of the world." When [Jesus] had said this, he spat on the ground and made mud with the saliva and spread the mud on the man's eyes, saying to him, "Go, wash in the pool of Siloam" (which means Sent). Then he went and washed and came back able to see.

To ponder

A woman whose husband had just died called me yesterday. She could not imagine why she would want to live and couldn't imagine how it would ever be different again. . . . I told her, "Someday this immense bottomless pit of pain will go away." It should be the work of Christians . . . to help people when they are being led into the darkness and the void. The believer has to tell those in pain

that this is not forever; there is a light and you will see it.
—Richard Rohr, *Everything Belongs: The Gift of Contemplative Prayer*

Living in hope

Imagine the spectacle of placing mud made with spit on someone's eyes. We are amazed to learn that the appearance of muddy eyes soon gave way to the joyful experience of a blind man seeing for the first time. This is how life often unfolds. Counselors and therapists may ask, "What would your life be like if the things we have been talking about got even worse?" This technique helps identify our deepest fears and anxieties. Once we can recognize and even name the things that trouble us, we may be able to see more clearly the paths that will lead us to healing, growth, change, and peace.

When we feel lost, confused, and afraid, God wants to deepen our trust in the light of Christ. Yes, the night may seem darkest just before the dawn of a new day, but we are people who live in hope. Today we thank God for the gift of hope that does not disappoint us.

Prayer

God of mystery, we can never fully understand the ways your power is working in our lives. Our doubts will come, but you have promised that your grace and truth will always work to strengthen our faith. Thank you for this faith that can sustain us when our days seem overwhelmed by fear and darkness. Amen.

March 2

John 9:8-10

The neighbors and those who had seen him before as a beggar began to ask, "Is this not the man who used to sit and beg?" Some were saying, "It is he." Others were saying, "No, but it is someone like him." He kept saying, "I am the man." But they kept asking him, "Then how were your eyes opened?"

To ponder

Remember that the Emerald City in *The Wonderful Wizard of Oz* isn't actually emerald . . . in L. Frank Baum's original book, Dorothy and the others are exhorted to put on "safety goggles" to protect their eyes. "If you do not . . . the brightness and glory of the Emerald City would blind you." . . . "But isn't everything here green?" asks Dorothy. "No more than in any other city," replies Oz.

"But my people have worn green glasses on their eyes so long that most of them think it really is an Emerald City."
—Michael Harris, *The End of Absence*

Amazing grace

How ironic that when the man born blind can finally see, his neighbors struggle to accept the reality of what has happened to him. It's as if they can only see him through the lenses of their rigid assumptions about his place and his potential within their community.

God's power to heal, inspire, and transform our lives may prove difficult for our friends and neighbors to understand. This goes to the core of what it means for someone to say, "I was blind, and now I see." Amazing grace can change everything about us. Don't be surprised when people are astounded by the ways God can bring about change in our hearts, our homes, and even our global communities.

Prayer

Holy God, we thank you for your faithfulness to all your people. When we are lost, you find us. When we are blinded by sin's power, your grace reveals new visions of what you have empowered us to become. Send your Holy Spirit to encourage us when people doubt our ability to change. Allow us to see with our own eyes the signs of Jesus' light in our world and in our hearts. Let us never doubt that the brightness of your glory can show us how to live more fully as your children. Amen.

March 3

John 9:35-38

Jesus heard that they had driven him out, and when he found [the man born blind], he said, "Do you believe in the Son of Man?" He answered, "And who is he, sir? Tell me, so that I may believe in him." Jesus said to him, "You have seen him, and the one speaking with you is he." He said, "Lord, I believe." And he worshiped him.

To ponder

Imagining the characteristics that . . . describe a congregation if it were a person may begin to explain how the living system of a church . . . has its own peculiar "personality."
—Kathleen S. Smith, *Stilling the Storm*

Jesus finds us

How many people end up in our churches because they are literally driven away from communities that reject and devalue them and toward congregations and other ministries that offer them acceptance and support through the love of Christ? Of course, the life we share with other Christians is seldom fully free of conflict: sometimes we enjoy "smooth sailing" only to find ourselves suddenly caught up in the tumult of "rough seas."

The good news is: Jesus finds us. The man born blind was driven away by religious leaders who were insulted by his newly inspired ability to speak up for himself. He was given not only sight, but also a sense of agency, identity, and empowerment. Jesus found him, and the man said, "I believe," and began to worship him. How wonderful it is to know that the Holy Spirit can give us, individually and collectively, a heart and a personality fully open to the joy of the Lord.

Prayer

Lord God Almighty, you are like no other. We find new life every time we celebrate your power to save. We praise you for giving us freedom to serve you in this world. Thank you for the light of your salvation. Thank you for the many ways you call us to worship in the name of Jesus. Amen.

March 4 / Lent 3

John 15:1-3

[Jesus said,] "I am the true vine, and my Father is the vinegrower. He removes every branch in me that bears no fruit. Every branch that bears fruit he prunes to make it bear more fruit. You have already been cleansed by the word that I have spoken to you."

To ponder

A garden requires patient labor and attention. . . . Plants do not grow merely to satisfy ambitions or to fulfill good intentions. They thrive because someone expended effort on them.
—Liberty Hyde Bailey, *Country Life in America*

Bearing fruit

Look at the reading from John 15:1-3 again. We might see these words from Jesus as threat and judgment, that God will make sure, whether you like it or not, that you are worthy of bearing fruit. But there is no such intimation in these verses. Among Jesus' last words to his disciples, they are meant to offer promise and hope. I am not much of a gardener, but I know that a little pruning here and there results in a greater yield. That's exactly what's at stake at this point for the disciples. Jesus is leaving, returning to his Father, so how will his mission to bring new life to the world be fulfilled? The answer is through those who believe in Jesus, through you and me.

Lent is a time for reflection, but not only on your own personal relationship with Jesus. Rather, Lent should be a time to contemplate the ways in which you actively participate in Jesus' mission. This is bearing fruit. Jesus calls us to think outside of ourselves as if the world depended on it, because it does. You see, God is not satisfied with being in relationship with only a few, but desires to love all. Are we willing to share our relationship with God with others?

Prayer

Jesus, help me to bear fruit that invites all into a relationship with you. Amen.

March 5

John 15:4-6

[Jesus said,] "Abide in me as I abide in you. Just as the branch cannot bear fruit by itself unless it abides in the vine, neither can you unless you abide in me. I am the vine, you are the branches. Those who abide in me and I in them bear much fruit, because apart from me you can do nothing. Whoever does not abide in me is thrown away like a branch and withers; such branches are gathered, thrown into the fire, and burned."

To ponder

A community that cannot empathize will never be able to discuss the difficult issues that divide it, and that divide society as a whole.

—Matthew L. Skinner, "Preaching in a Time of Political Anxiety"

Abide in me

It is no accident that the last image Jesus uses for himself and his disciples is a vine with its branches. In fact, this last "I am" statement in John is all about Jesus' relationship with his followers. That should make us pause. It should also remind us of the previous "I am" statements: *I am the bread of life. I am the light of the world. I am the good shepherd. I am the living water. I am the resurrection and the life.*

Pondering the meaning of "I am the vine, you are the branches" in light of the other statements reminds us that Jesus is the source of our provision, the source of our protection, the source of life itself. And notice that Jesus does not say, "Be the branches," but "You are the branches." This is Jesus' promise to us.

Prayer

Dear Jesus, thank you for reminding us of your constant care for, and presence in, our lives. Amen.

March 6

John 15:7-8

[Jesus continued,] "If you abide in me, and my words abide in you, ask for whatever you wish, and it will be done for you. My Father is glorified by this, that you bear much fruit and become my disciples."

To ponder

I was happy to help [Isaiah Thomas]. He had the courage to ask. I did the same thing with Michael Jordan when I was a young player. —Kobe Bryant, *Slam Online*

The courage to ask

Jesus' invitation to ask for whatever we wish is easily misinterpreted and misused. It can become a free pass for making requests that are never quite fair and assume a certain control over God. We can easily fall into this trap, acting as if our relationship with God is a mere contract to get what we want. God becomes a "back pocket" deity whom we pull out when we need to, but are quite content to keep out of sight when a transaction is not immediately necessary. What God has done for us for eternity becomes less important than "What have you done for me lately?"

The invitation to ask, however, needs to be heard within a relationship of dependence. It emphasizes that the disciples' relationship with Jesus and with God is real. Although the disciples will have many needs when Jesus is gone, his physical absence will not jeopardize the unity they have with him and with God. Ask away, not for the sake of getting what you want, but because asking is possible only within a relationship of trust.

Prayer

Dear God, today we pray for the courage to ask because it comes from trust in your love. Amen.

March 7

John 15:9-11

[Jesus said,] "As the Father has loved me, so I have loved you; abide in my love. If you keep my commandments, you will abide in my love, just as I have kept my Father's commandments and abide in his love. I have said these things to you so that my joy may be in you, and that your joy may be complete."

To ponder

Goodbyes can be poignant, sorrowful, sometimes a relief, and now and then, an occasion for joy. They are always transition moments which, when embraced, can be the door to a new life both for ourselves and for others.

—Roger Housden, "Seeing the Good in Goodbyes"

Joy

Joy amid impending separation and goodbyes? How is this possible, especially during Lent? Lent is traditionally a time for somber contemplation, for appropriate restraint and reserve. Joy seems out of place, even sacrilegious. To be appropriately penitential, we tend to ignore the reference to joy in John 15, as if experiencing joy in this season of repentance would be displeasing to God.

Yet if we stop to think about it, Jesus is speaking a truth about life. Memorable moments often are simultaneously filled with both grief and glory. A graduation, for example, is a goodbye, but also a time of anticipation, excitement, and joy. That morning when your oldest son comes down the stairs and realizes he is finally taller than you prompts both sadness for what's gone and happiness upon seeing his beaming smile.

Farewells can also be events that recall, relive, and reimagine joy. Yes, Jesus is leaving. Jesus will die. But the joy that he and the disciples have experienced up to this point is a joy they will continue to know. Joy is indeed a promise of discipleship.

Prayer

God, when we are tempted to see only heartache and suffering, remind us that your joy will carry us through. Amen.

March 8

John 15:12-14

[Jesus continued,] "This is my commandment, that you love one another as I have loved you. No one has greater love than this, to lay down one's life for one's friends. You are my friends if you do what I command you."

To ponder

Love is the only force capable of transforming an enemy into a friend. —Martin Luther King Jr., *Strength to Love*

Will you lay down your life?

Jesus lays down his life for the disciples, for us—and he expects us to do the same for others, for each other? Well, that's a difficult pill to swallow. Our inclination is to make these kinds of statements less unpleasant or offensive. Jesus didn't literally mean dying for our friends, right? It was more of a metaphor, a suggestion, easily tamed by our reluctance to imagine that discipleship just might require some sacrifice. At the same time, we are easily convinced that we can heroically live up to this expectation, but we can't do what Jesus did. Let's be clear about that. None of us are able to do what Jesus did on the cross.

Jesus stood up to powers that exclude, powers that demoralize, powers that silence. We can lay down our lives for those whom power marginalizes, dehumanizes, and shuts up. We can lay down our lives for those who wonder when they will have their next meal, who will hold them in the dark, who will welcome them when all they have known is rejection. A quick review of the Gospel of John up to this point reveals that Jesus has been laying down his life all along. We are called to do the same.

Prayer

Dear God, enable me to see those in my life who need me to lay down my life so that they might have life. Amen.

March 9

John 15:15

[Jesus said,] "I do not call you servants any longer, because the servant does not know what the master is doing; but I have called you friends, because I have made known to you everything that I have heard from my Father."

To ponder

Jesus does not merely talk the language of friendship; he lives out his life and death as friend.

—Gail O'Day, "Jesus as Friend in the Gospel of John"

What a friend we have in Jesus

Let's be clear. The expectations of friendship with Jesus aren't equivalent to common assumptions about friendship in today's society. Jesus doesn't promise to be your BFF. Nor does Jesus have in mind being your Facebook friend. You don't get to "unfriend" or "unfollow" Jesus when times get tough.

Friendship in the ancient world demanded certain commitments and structures, as well as faithfulness. For Jesus and the disciples, a master-servant relationship had worked just fine when the disciples had some following and some learning to do. But in John 15, everything changes. Jesus uses friendship as a model to help the disciples reimagine their relationship with him. They can no longer be servants or pupils; they are called to be Jesus' presence in the world.

To be Jesus' friend is to embody commitment, responsibility, and accountability. Now more than ever, Jesus needs his friends—you and me—to make known to others what he has made known to us.

Prayer

Dear Jesus, thank you for being my friend, for making me your friend. I love you. Amen.

March 10

John 15:16-17

[Jesus said,] "You did not choose me but I chose you. And I appointed you to go and bear fruit, fruit that will last, so that the Father will give you whatever you ask him in my name. I am giving you these commands so that you may love one another."

To ponder

Worry does not empty tomorrow of its sorrow; it empties today of its strength.

—Corrie ten Boom, in *A Theological Miscellany* by T. J. McTavish

Choose me

God chooses us? Really? We could easily come up with reasons why this simply cannot be true, and we would be in good company. Look at two of the many examples in scripture. Moses insisted that God could not possibly be right in choosing him. How could he go up against the Egyptian pharaoh when he had not yet taken a course in public speaking? Jeremiah told God, "Thanks, but I'm kind of young for what you have in mind. Let me get a little experience under my belt, and then ask me again sometime." God responded to every excuse from Moses and Jeremiah and sent them out with messages to deliver.

Jesus chose his disciples and called them to follow him. Philip was minding his own business when Jesus found him, and then Philip found Nathanael and brought him to Jesus. That's what it means to "go and bear fruit." Jesus finds you and you find others, because Jesus has other sheep that are not of this fold (John 10:16)—and it just so happens that God loves the world. We may be full of reasons why we are not enough for this mission or for God. But God will reject every excuse and insist, *I chose you. You are enough and I need you.*

Prayer

Dear God, help me to believe that I am enough and you choose me. Amen.

March 11 / Lent 4

John 4:7, 25-26

A Samaritan woman came to draw water, and Jesus said to her, "Give me a drink." . . .

The woman said to him, "I know that Messiah is coming" (who is called Christ). "When he comes, he will proclaim all things to us." Jesus said to her, "I am he, the one who is speaking to you."

To ponder

Instructions for living a life.
Pay attention.
Be astonished.
Tell about it.
—Mary Oliver, "Sometimes"

I AM

Take out a pen (or a pencil, if it makes you nervous to cross out words in the Bible) and put an X through the "he" that follows "I am" in John 4:26. There is no "he" in the Greek text of the New Testament. Why does this matter? Because this is the first time in the Gospel of John that Jesus reveals his true identity. He really is the Word made flesh (John 1:14), God incarnate, the "I AM" God of Moses (Exodus 3:13-15). And to whom does Jesus first disclose who he truly is? Not to the disciples. Not to the religious elite. Not to those in power. No, Jesus shares his true self with the last person on the face of the planet whom people would have thought God could love. This woman. This Samaritan. With no name, no credibility, no respect.

How much we are like her. Really, why would Jesus want to talk to me? Value me? See me as someone who might witness to the very persons who have rejected me; who leave me alone to fetch water at the high heat of the day; who say, "Girlfriend, that is some bad luck you've had—I don't want it to rub off on me." But Jesus speaks to the Samaritan woman and she returns to the city telling people, "Come and see this man."

Prayer

Dear God, when I doubt that I am worthy of love and belonging, come to me again and say, "I AM." Amen.

March 12

John 6:16-20

When evening came, his disciples went down to the sea, got into a boat, and started across the sea to Capernaum. It was now dark, and Jesus had not yet come to them. The sea became rough because a strong wind was blowing. When they had rowed about three or four miles, they saw Jesus walking on the sea and coming near the boat, and they were terrified. But he said to them, "It is I; do not be afraid."

To ponder

Our deepest fear is not that we are inadequate. Our deepest fear is that we are powerful beyond measure. . . . We were born to make manifest the glory of God that is within us. It's not just in some of us; it's in everyone. —Marianne Williamson, *A Return to Love*

What are we afraid of?

This is one of those times when things get lost in translation. The more accurate translation of "It is I" in John 6:20 is "I AM." There are two kinds of "I am" statements in the Gospel of John: statements that equate Jesus with an image or object (for example, "I am the bread of life"), and what we call the absolute "I AM" statements in which Jesus lets us know just who he really is (John 4:26; 6:20; 8:24, 28, 58; 13:19; 18:5, 8).

This is the first time that the disciples hear an absolute "I AM" from Jesus, and it comes at a significant point. First, the sea was not seen as a friendly place by people in the ancient world. The source of their livelihood could also, in a heartbeat, take away life. The disciples are terrified when Jesus shows up. Second, in John's gospel this stormy episode comes after the feeding of the five thousand and just before Jesus' revelation that he is the bread of life. We might say the feeding of the five thousand is just the kind of thing God does. But there's more to it than that. In the wilderness, God gave the Israelites manna from heaven and water from rocks. In Jesus, God is once again present and providing for God's people.

Prayer

God, you show up when we most need it and when we least expect it. Thank you for keeping your promises. Amen.

March 13

John 8:23-26

[Jesus] said to them, "You are from below, I am from above; you are of this world, I am not of this world. I told you that you would die in your sins, for you will die in your sins unless you believe that I am he." They said to him, "Who are you?" Jesus said to them, "Why do I speak to you at all? I have much to say about you and much to condemn; but the one who sent me is true, and I declare to the world what I have heard from him."

To ponder

You are imperfect, you are wired for struggle, but you are worthy of love and belonging.

—Brené Brown, "The Power of Vulnerability"

Who are you?

In today's text from John 8, Jesus is speaking to the Jewish leaders. Taken out of context, Jesus' words sound harsh, but this passage gives us a rare glimpse into first-century debates about the interpretation of scripture and the activity of God. Jesus is not condemning Judaism—he is a Jew. But he is challenging the powers that have usurped imagination of what God could be doing in the world. The leaders are resisting a possible relationship with God. And why? Because this relationship is being offered outside of their comfortable and familiar boundaries.

How often we do the same. We limit our expectations of God or put boundaries and constraints on where God is at work. The season of Lent reminds us that as much as we want God, need God, to match our image of who we expect God to be, that will all be upended. "Who is Jesus?" is the central question. How will you answer?

Prayer

God, we know who you are because of Jesus. We pray today that we might actually believe it. Amen.

March 14

John 8:28-30

So Jesus said, "When you have lifted up the Son of Man, then you will realize that I am he, and that I do nothing on my own, but I speak these things as the Father instructed me. And the one who sent me is with me; he has not left me alone, for I always do what is pleasing to him." As he was saying these things, many believed in him.

To ponder

The Bible's inclusion of so many figures for God is both an invitation and a caution. The invitation to discovery: discovery of who God is. . . . The caution is against assuming that any one image of God . . . adequately describes God.

—Lauren Winner, *Wearing God*

Lifted up

Here we have another "I AM" statement from Jesus. This time
Jesus says we will know he is I AM when he has been "lifted up."
What does this "lifting up" mean? All too quickly, we might
assume that the moment Jesus is lifted up is the crucifixion. The
cross makes sense here, and we are in the season of Lent, after
all. The cross is central to who Jesus was and is and who we need
Jesus to be.

Yes, Jesus is lifted up at the moment of his crucifixion. Yet in
the Gospel of John, there's more to the story. Jesus will also be
lifted at his resurrection and again at his ascension. In other
words, Jesus' identity is not just about his death, but also about
his resurrection and ascension. In the crucifixion, we realize that
Jesus is really one of us. Flesh and blood. One who died not just
for us, but because he became one of us. In the resurrection, we
see that death is not the end. God upends even death. In the
ascension, we realize that the fullest experience of a relationship
with God is a deep and intimate abiding. All three scenes together
give us a fuller picture of who Jesus is.

Prayer

Dear God, lift up our hearts to see that in your death, your resurrection, and your ascension you draw us deeper into a relationship with you. Amen.

March 15

John 8:56-59

[Jesus said,] "Your ancestor Abraham rejoiced that he would see my day; he saw it and was glad." Then the Jews said to him, "You are not yet fifty years old, and have you seen Abraham?" Jesus said to them, "Very truly, I tell you, before Abraham was, I am." So they picked up stones to throw at him, but Jesus hid himself and went out of the temple.

To ponder

When I live believing my life is the only life that matters, God, remind me that the faces of others reflect your face, the struggles of others bring your liberation to my life, and the kindness of others speaks your grace into my soul.

—Bruce Reyes-Chow, *40 Days, 40 Prayers, 40 Words*

Love without limits

It's not surprising that the Jewish leaders picked up stones to throw at Jesus. To begin with, Abraham was the father of the faith, who birthed the nation of Israel. When Jesus claims he existed even before Abraham (see John 1:1), it sounds absurd to the Jewish leaders. Adding fuel to the proverbial fire, at this point in the conversation, Jesus has stated three times that he is "I AM." When someone intimates that he is God, not once but three times, this could be cause for consternation, to say the least. After all, the essential claim of Judaism was that there is one God. Jesus challenges both the role of Abraham and the one God who called Abraham in the first place.

What does all of this mean for us? No one gets to keep God for themselves. Being a child of God is open to all, not just to descendants of Abraham. Jesus' death, resurrection, and ascension took place to draw all people to God (John 12:32).

Prayer

Dear God, when we try to limit your love, remind us that your love is for the world. Amen.

March 16

John 13:18-20

[Jesus said,] "I am not speaking of all of you; I know whom I have chosen. But it is to fulfill the scripture, 'The one who ate my bread has lifted his heel against me.' I tell you this now, before it occurs, so that when it does occur, you may believe that I am he. Very truly, I tell you, whoever receives one whom I send receives me; and whoever receives me receives him who sent me."

To ponder

The whole purpose of the Bible, it seems to me, is to convince people to set the written word down in order to become living words in the world for God's sake.
—Barbara Brown Taylor, *Leaving Church*

Betrayal

Jesus washes the feet of the disciples. He hasn't yet mentioned that one of them will betray him. Then he reminds the disciples who he is. Between unity and division, between community and fracture, between commitment and desertion comes this reminder at just the right time, exactly when we need to hear it, because we could so easily forget how challenging it is to follow Jesus. This is what Jesus does, you know. Interrupts, intercedes, and inserts himself and his truth in our lives because our tendency is to pass over those places where difficulty in believing God outweighs the promises of God. Following Jesus is not for the faint of heart and does not suffer fools lightly.

In the end, Judas's betrayal will not be the handing over of Jesus. Jesus does that on his own in John's gospel, willingly stepping out of the garden because the good shepherd lays down his own life and no one will take it from him. Rather, in his betrayal of Jesus, Judas rejects the relationship Jesus offers with himself, with God, and with the community committed to witnessing that Jesus is the Word made flesh. How do you respond to the challenging invitation to follow Jesus?

Prayer

Jesus, please continue to show up and say "I AM," especially when I need to hear it the most. Amen.

March 17

John 18:3-8

So Judas brought a detachment of soldiers together with police from the chief priests and the Pharisees, and they came [to the garden] with lanterns and torches and weapons. Then Jesus, knowing all that was to happen to him, came forward and asked them, "Whom are you looking for?" They answered, "Jesus of Nazareth." Jesus replied, "I am he." Judas, who betrayed him, was standing with them. When Jesus said to them, "I am he," they stepped back and fell to the ground. Again he asked them, "Whom are you looking for?" And they said, "Jesus of Nazareth." Jesus answered, "I told you that I am he."

To ponder

The quest for aliveness is the best thing about religion, I think. It's what we are hoping for when we pray. It's why we gather, celebrate, eat, abstain, practice, sing, and contemplate.
— Brian D. McLaren, *We Make the Road by Walking*

Awe and aliveness

The absolute "I AM" statements in John 18 are the last ones in the gospel, and they are for the world to hear, the world God so loves. Jesus' claim of "I AM" causes a detachment of soldiers (equivalent to 600 men in the Roman army) to fall back in the face of God's presence. This is what happens when God shows up. There is no other response but to step back and fall to the ground in sheer wonder and awe and even terror.

"Whom are you looking for?" is the essential question of Lent. If you are looking for a God who tries to find an out, who uses power to yield a more favorable personal result, who abandons the cause when life is at stake, then you need to look elsewhere. This God will hand God's self over, will be arrested and bound, and will be tried and crucified. This God inspires wonder and awe and aliveness. Whom are you looking for?

Prayer

Dear God, the one I am looking for is really, truly you. Please show me where and how this is true. Amen.

March 18 / Lent 5

John 6:31-32

[The crowd said,] "Our ancestors ate the manna in the wilderness; as it is written, 'He gave them bread from heaven to eat.'" Then Jesus said to them, "Very truly, I tell you, it was not Moses who gave you the bread from heaven, but it is my Father who gives you the true bread from heaven."

To ponder

My mother reached up and put her hand gently on his shoulder and Jake cleared his throat and tried again. "Heavenly Father, for the blessings of this food and these friends and our families, we thank you. In Jesus's name, amen." That was it. That was all of it. A grace so ordinary there was no reason at all to remember it. Yet

I have never across the forty years since it was spoken forgotten a single word." —William Kent Krueger, *Ordinary Grace*

Falling grace

The snow had fallen all night, so that we awoke to more than a foot blanketing everything. The children rushed to get on their snow gear, eager to jump, slide, build, and taste the magic of this cold, white stuff falling from the sky.

Too soon, the lovely snow had melted or transformed to a gray, sooty mush. The children's interest waned. The snowfall became a thing of the past, a memory until the next time the heavens open and all seems new and fresh once more.

Did you notice in John's gospel the shift in grammatical tense? Moses gave, my Father gives. Give us this day our daily bread, we pray. This moment, though remembered, reveals God's presence. Unlike the new fallen snow or the manna, God's grace does not perish with the day, but endures forever.

Throughout our lives, we can recall moments of ordinary grace: the presence of a friend, special meals, or an unexpected gift from a stranger. We might call it fate, but looking back, we see God at work, giving us grace that overwhelms us with beauty, that tastes as fresh as new fallen snow.

Prayer

God of grace, give us the wonder of a child, that we may be amazed at the ordinary goodness we encounter this day. Amen.

March 19

John 6:33-34

[Jesus said,] "For the bread of God is that which comes down from heaven and gives life to the world." They said to him, "Sir, give us this bread always."

To ponder

All that grounded me were those pieces of bread. I was feeling my way toward a theology, beginning with what I had taken in my mouth and working it out from there.
—Sara Miles, *Take This Bread*

Tasting is believing

They say seeing is believing.

Many years ago, my spouse accompanied me to dinner and we ordered the food I had been craving: sushi. He had yet to try it and decided the time had arrived. We ordered the entry-level California roll served with the traditional sides, one of them being a pale green paste. My husband noticed it, and thinking it was mashed avocado, he ate a forkful! If you have ever tasted wasabi, you could predict the response: the shock at this tremendously spicy food, the nasal passages painfully awoken. Perhaps the common phrase should be revised: tasting is believing.

Seeing food spread out before us can be a feast for the eyes, but it is in the tasting that we understand, that we remember. We want to trust our eyes, but to know something deeply in our bodies, we taste.

Followers of Jesus believe that divine love comes so close to us we can taste it. We believe in Jesus not because we have seen him; we have not. We can believe, though, because we have tasted him in the bread we share. And this tasting like no other brings life for the world.

Prayer

Giver of bread, you dwell in us. May we always taste and see that you are good. Amen.

March 20

John 6:35

Jesus said to them, "I am the bread of life. Whoever comes to me will never be hungry, and whoever believes in me will never be thirsty."

To ponder

God says, "I do not chose to come to you in my majesty and in the company of angels but in the guise of a poor beggar asking for bread. . . . I want you to know that I am the one who is suffering hunger and thirst."
—Martin Luther, "Sermon on the Gospel of St. John" (1540)

Hunger

"I'm starving." Every time those words escape my mouth or the mouths of my children, I bristle. A tummy rumble? Sure. A hunger headache? Okay. But my family and I are not starving.

People all over the world are starving. The United Nations Food and Agriculture Organization estimates that about 795 million people of the 7.3 billion people in the world, or one in nine, were suffering from chronic undernourishment from 2014 to 2016.

How can we digest a statistic like this when Jesus promises that no one will be hungry or thirsty if they come to him? It can be tempting to cast aside real hunger and focus instead on spiritual hunger. Yet we believe in a God who took on flesh in a human being who felt hunger. For Jesus on the cross, thirst was no abstraction.

This hungering Jesus also commands his disciples then and now to "give them something to eat" (Matthew 14:16). Walking in the way of Jesus, the hungering one, we reach out our hands to help all who hunger.

Prayer

God of abundance, fill those who hunger and awaken your church to the needs of hungry people everywhere. Amen.

March 21

John 6:48-50

[Jesus said,] "I am the bread of life. Your ancestors ate manna in the wilderness, and they died. This is the bread that comes down from heaven, so that one may eat of it and not die."

To ponder

Poets tell us what our eyes, blurred with too much gawking, and our ears, dull with too much chatter, miss around and within us. Poets use words to drag us into the depths of reality itself. Poetry grabs us by the jugular; far from being cosmetic language, it is intestinal.

—Eugene Peterson, interview for *On Being* radio show and podcast

Be our bread

For four days we have been meditating upon the sixth chapter of John's gospel and Jesus has said twice, "I am the bread of life." The verses are poetic, steeped in metaphor. But if poetry just sounded pretty, we would adorn the Bible in a glass case and admire it from afar. Instead, we are caught up in the messiness of metaphor.

When we first hear Jesus is bread, we might think, "Sure, that sounds good. We like thinking about Jesus as food that tastes good." Then we realize, "No, that's not true. People aren't bread; God isn't bread. Bread is flour and yeast, liquid, salt, and sweetener."

But finally, yes, like bread, we need Jesus. Our bodies need Jesus. Without a relationship with God, we wander in the wilderness, grasping for stuff we think gives life but eventually fails. Loved ones who have cared for us desert us, break our hearts, and die. The stuff we amass crowds our closets and basements. We pay rent for extra boxes to store the excess. Even the food we love only fills us for so long. The next day, we will be hungry. Yes, Jesus, you are the bread of life.

Prayer

God, our life, our bread, open us to the power of poetry in our relationship with you and the world you love. Amen.

March 22

John 6:51-52

[Jesus said,] "I am the living bread that came down from heaven. Whoever eats of this bread will live forever; and the bread that I will give for the life of the world is my flesh." The Jews then disputed among themselves, saying, "How can this man give us his flesh to eat?"

To ponder

To live, we must daily break the body and shed the blood of creation. —Wendell Berry, *The Gift of Good Land*

Caring creatures

I'll never forget my college foray into vegetarianism. My husband's sister raised Polled Herefords. She lovingly cared for these cattle in the way we understand the "husband" in animal husbandry. This did not change their purpose, though, as beef cattle. One summer evening as the family gathered for a steak dinner, I learned that the meal's meat came from a cow that shared the same name as my husband. After my making small strides toward eating no meat, this naming sealed the deal. No more steak!

I am no longer a vegetarian, but vegetarian or not, it is important for us as human creatures to wrestle with how the earth is broken and shed for our existence. What is the source of our meat? What about the condition of animals in factory farms and workers in packing plants? Do farmers exposed to pesticides pay in disease what we save in cents at the store? And the questions continue, asking so much because so much is broken in the name of life. Christians rightly ask these questions because we believe that our creation has been called "very good," a promise sealed by Christ's being broken and shed for us.

Prayer

Source of all, be patient with our questions and searching on this journey to love your creation as you intend. Amen.

March 23

John 6:53-56

So Jesus said to them, "Very truly, I tell you, unless you eat the flesh of the Son of Man and drink his blood, you have no life in you. Those who eat my flesh and drink my blood have eternal life, and I will raise them up on the last day; for my flesh is true food and my blood is true drink. Those who eat my flesh and drink my blood abide in me, and I in them."

To ponder

Christ, Bread of heaven, / Rise in us sweetly, / Fill us with beauty, / So that your people / With your compassion / Leaven creation.
—Susan Palo Cherwien, "Christ, Burning Wisdom"

Just abide

A recent blog post making the rounds on social media called busyness a disease. In extreme cases of busyness, abiding is all but impossible. Most of us have likely succumbed to this disease, experiencing the symptoms of restlessness. How can we dwell when we can't settle down?

Baking bread takes time: warming the liquid, proofing the yeast, mixing the ingredients into a dough, and waiting. Then more and more waiting for the yeast and sweetener to do their work while we go about other tasks. Yes, baking bread takes time for mixing and kneading, not to mention washing the dough-encrusted bowl, but the majority of the time is simply waiting. You need to be home to do it, but mostly just hanging out, abiding.

This Lent, can we take some time to notice God's patient rising in us? Even if we can't bake bread, perhaps taking those moments to offer thanks for the bread helps us acknowledge God's patient homemaking with us.

Prayer

Abiding God, thank you for making your home with us and with the whole creation. Amen.

March 24

John 6:57-58

[Jesus said,] "Just as the living Father sent me, and I live because of the Father, so whoever eats me will live because of me. This is the bread that came down from heaven, not like that which your ancestors ate, and they died. But the one who eats this bread will live forever."

To ponder

Eternal vigor, Saving One, / you free us by your living Word, / becoming flesh to wear our pain, / and all creation is restored.
—Jean Janzen, "O Holy Spirit, Root of Life"

Vigorous restoration

Could life with God be described as vigorous restoration? *Vigorous* means energetic, vital, spirited. *Restoration* means repair, renewal. Human beings and the earth we call home are caught up in this power of God that energizes and renews.

How many times have you looked on in wonder as a child runs or climbs at full speed yet shows no signs of tiring? "I wish I had their energy," you remark. Scripture tells us that those who do not receive the kingdom of God like a child will never enter it. Does this mean we need to climb on the furniture and tear down the hallway? Probably not. But perhaps it means that we have energy, however diminished. Part of being a person of faith means trusting that energy we call the Holy Spirit.

Like a garment, we will wear out. But we are promised that God's vigor will keep on working, keep on running and climbing, never giving up on us when we have given up on ourselves. By faith, we trust in God's promise of restoration.

Prayer

Spirit of life, enliven our flesh with your endless supply of energy. Amen.

March 25 / Sunday of the Passion

John 11:17-22

When Jesus arrived, he found that Lazarus had already been in the tomb four days. Now Bethany was near Jerusalem, some two miles away, and many of the Jews had come to Martha and Mary to console them about their brother. When Martha heard that Jesus was coming, she went and met him, while Mary stayed at home. Martha said to Jesus, "Lord, if you had been here, my brother would not have died. But even now I know that God will give you whatever you ask of him."

To ponder

Perhaps contradictions are not impediments to the spiritual life but an integral part of it. Through them we may learn that the

power for life comes from God, not from us.
—Parker Palmer, *The Promise of Paradox*

Both/and

Psychologists teach us about the five stages of grief first proposed by Elisabeth Kübler-Ross in her 1969 book *On Death and Dying*: denial, anger, bargaining, depression, and acceptance. Each of us moves in and out of these stages in no particular order and for various lengths of time.

With that in mind, read again the account of Martha who mourns the loss of her brother and Mary who stays home. Do you hear some bargaining and anger in Martha's first address to Jesus? "If you had been here!" What seems utterly remarkable is the next sentence, her utmost confidence in God granting Jesus whatever she asks. It's as if she moves through the stages of grief within the span of two sentences!

On this day, the church celebrates Palm/Passion Sunday. "Hosanna" and "Crucify" both come from our lips. Some may struggle with this juxtaposition; it seems disjointed to move from laud and honor to despair and shame. But Martha reveals that our lives are like that, moving from doubt to acceptance in a breath. We enter this Holy Week trusting that no matter the depths of our grief or heights of our belief, Jesus walks with us.

Prayer

Hear, O God, our rejoicing and our suffering, that in every stage of life, you are our hope and salvation. Amen.

March 26

John 11:23-27

Jesus said to her, "Your brother will rise again." Martha said to him, "I know that he will rise again in the resurrection on the last day." Jesus said to her, "I am the resurrection and the life. Those who believe in me, even though they die, will live, and everyone who lives and believes in me will never die. Do you believe this?" She said to him, "Yes, Lord, I believe that you are the Messiah, the Son of God, the one coming into the world."

To ponder

"We delight in the beauty of a butterfly, but rarely admit the changes it has gone through to achieve that beauty."
—Maya Angelou, "When I Sense"

84

Springing forth

Ants swarming on the crack in the sidewalk. Bits of tree blossom blown by the wind and scattered on the street. Robins digging for a worm in the dirt. All of these in central Pennsylvania point to spring, signs that winter has come to an end and warm summer days lie ahead.

When we see new life around us, it can be easy to forget that winter, too, has its beauty. Plants enter dormant states and animals hibernate in preparation for what comes next; much is happening, even if we can't see it or appreciate it.

It can be easy to marvel at the beautiful butterfly or rejoice in joyful times. Yet we who share Martha's faith in the Messiah know the whole story. We behold Christ's beauty scarred by suffering and rejoice in one who was buried to spring forth. As one Easter hymn announces: "Love is come again like wheat arising green" (ELW 379). This is the way to which Christ calls: abundant life in season and out of season.

Prayer

Give us faith, God of beauty, to believe in life springing from death. Amen.

March 27

John 11:32-33

When Mary came where Jesus was and saw him, she knelt at his feet and said to him, "Lord, if you had been here, my brother would not have died." When Jesus saw her weeping, and the Jews who came with her also weeping, he was greatly disturbed in spirit and deeply moved.

To ponder

And tears came before he could stop them, boiling hot then instantly freezing on his face, and what was the point in wiping them off? Or pretending? He let them fall.
—J. K. Rowling, *Harry Potter and the Deathly Hallows*

If only . . .

Everyone is weeping. In tomorrow's passage from John, we'll get a little further in the story and discover that even Jesus weeps. No one steps in saying, "Stop your crying already." No, they just cry.

Can you hear the Marys crying today for losses they hoped to prevent? If only I had realized he was so depressed, I wouldn't have let him have that gun. If only I hadn't sent that text while driving, he would still be alive. If only I could have blocked the shooter from entering the school, the club, the mall, the movie theater. If only I hadn't drunk so much. If only . . .

In all the "if only" moments, you know the most comforting response is not that "everything will be okay." No, it won't. At least not right away. If anything can bring comfort, it comes when someone kneels close by, putting an arm around your shoulders and crying with you. Gathered together, let the tears fall. God can take it.

Prayer

Weep with us, O God, when sorrow fills us to overflowing. Amen.

March 28

John 11:34-38

[Jesus] said, "Where have you laid him?" They said to him, "Lord, come and see." Jesus began to weep. So the Jews said, "See how he loved him!" But some of them said, "Could not he who opened the eyes of the blind man have kept this man from dying?" Then Jesus, again greatly disturbed, came to the tomb. It was a cave, and a stone was lying against it.

To ponder

The tears of God are the meaning of history.
—Nicholas Wolterstorff, *Lament for a Son*

God, our friend

You might be familiar with the nineteenth-century gospel hymn "What a Friend We Have in Jesus." Have you ever stopped to think about that line or other lines from scripture that call Jesus a friend?

Here at the tomb, Jesus reveals his deep friendship with Lazarus. He wants to know where he is; those around Jesus can see that he loved Lazarus very much. But even Jesus, a great friend, couldn't stop his friend from dying, at least not in the way we'd expect.

As a friend, you want to be physically present when your friend suffers or struggles. You're pained when you can't be near them. You so love your friend.

It seems beyond comprehension that our faith rests in a God who stoops to us as a friend, who calls us not servants but friends, who cherishes us in this relationship not of birth and blood, but of accompaniment and love.

Who are the friends who walk this Lenten journey with you? How might you "come and see" together this God who calls you a friend?

Prayer

God, our friend in Jesus, open our hearts to your holy comfort. Amen.

March 29 / Maundy Thursday

John 11:39-40

Jesus said, "Take away the stone." Martha, the sister of the dead man, said to him, "Lord, already there is a stench because he has been dead four days." Jesus said to her, "Did I not tell you that if you believed, you would see the glory of God?"

To ponder

Air and light heal; they somehow get into those dark, musty places, like spiritual antibiotics.
—Anne Lamott, *Help, Thanks, Wow*

Light in the darkness

Realists tell it like it is: "That stinks." Sometimes it is meant literally. Maybe the fridge hasn't been cleaned in too long. The compost bin overflows with rotten fruit. The downstairs basement has been sealed up and in the corner lies a rotting mouse. Decay smells.

In our 21st-century culture, death has been industrialized and sanitized to the point where most of us don't smell it. Yet the rediscovery of "green" burial practices often includes the family being with a dead body, tenderly washing and caring for their loved one. Then, instead of being protected in layers of steel or other metals, the body is buried in a simple shroud or pine box that is not airtight. Light will seep through.

When buried in fabric or wood rather than steel or stone, bodies will be changed by wind and sun; they will not be perfectly preserved. This might be too hard for us to take in, but what if we believe that glory really does come from God even in the midst of death? Even when we try to seal away death in the dark, do we trust that darkness brings forth light and life?

Prayer

Living God, renew our faith in Jesus, whose Spirit makes all things new. Amen.

March 30 / Good Friday

John 11:41-42

So they took away the stone. And Jesus looked upward and said, "Father, I thank you for having heard me. I knew that you always hear me, but I have said this for the sake of the crowd standing here, so that they may believe that you sent me."

To ponder

We pray for other people, bringing to God the needs of everyone we can think of. It is as if in this prayer, we imagine ourselves with the small circle of people at the foot of the cross; but encountering God's love for us, we realize that our circle of care must grow ever wider . . . centered at the cross, we see our arms always expanding to embrace more of the world.

—Gail Ramshaw, *The Three-Day Feast*

Prayers abounding

The church gathers on Ash Wednesday, the beginning of Lent, to hear words about praying in secret from Matthew's gospel. Now on Good Friday, we hear that Jesus prays not only for his heavenly Father to hear him, but also that others might believe. What seemed a private moment becomes a public work.

The Good Friday liturgy contains the ancient bidding prayer, a lengthy prayer for the needs of the world. In our congregation one year, we had an eager acolyte who didn't have many responsibilities for that particular service. During a worship service when some might extinguish candles, casting the church into somber darkness, this acolyte stood behind a small table containing ten small votive candles. An icon of the crucified Christ stood in front of the table. As we prayed each petition of the bidding prayer, he lit another candle, spreading light as we added prayers for the world God so loves.

Praying certainly expresses our faith, but we can also come to faith through prayer. When we name our needs before God, we are reminded that, yes, God cares for these needs. Like the crowd gathered around the praying Jesus, by hearing, we believe.

Prayer

Assure us, listening God, that when we ask in prayer, you never fail to hear us. Amen.

John 11:43-44

[Jesus] cried with a loud voice, "Lazarus, come out!" The dead man came out, his hands and feet bound with strips of cloth, and his face wrapped in a cloth. Jesus said to them, "Unbind him, and let him go."

To ponder

In even the best of caskets, it never all fits—all that we'd like to bury in them: the hurt and forgiveness, the anger and pain, the praise and thanksgiving, the emptiness and exaltations, the untidy feelings when someone dies.

—Thomas Lynch, *The Undertaking: Life Studies from the Dismal Trade*

Between the shores

"Let my people go," calls out the refrain of the African American spiritual "Go Down, Moses." The Israelites escaped their bondage under Pharaoh. Modern slavery was abolished in our country, yet so many are still enslaved by something or someone. The calls to be unbound echo still. Do we hear them?

On this day between crucifixion and resurrection, we discover the "already/not yet" dimension of our freedom in Christ. We claim that our dying and rising with Christ means freedom: freedom from the need to save ourselves. Yet we can't bury everything that binds us. Attempts to bury it all often leave us hollow like the tomb Lazarus has left. While we are promised freedom, it often feels like one foot has crossed the sea while the other remains stuck on the shore. Underneath is this raging water; we fear for our lives.

Easter promises us that we can actually just jump in the water, the waters of our baptism. This is the way of Jesus, the way of freedom. Though life brings tumultuous waves, the same Spirit who called Jesus beloved calls us beloved and lets us go to love and serve. Alleluia!

Prayer

Free us, living God, to be people of the Way: your way of justice, love, and mercy. Amen.

Notes

February 14: Amelia Boynton Robinson, *Bridge across Jordan* (Schiller Institute, 1991). **February 15:** Robert Frost, "The Road Not Taken," *Mountain Interval* (Henry Holt and Company, 1916). **February 16:** Frances Burney, *The Early Journals and Letters of Fanny Burney*, vol. 1, ed. Lars E. Troide (McGill-Queens University Press, 1988), 69. **February 17:** Mother Teresa, in *Stories Told by Mother Teresa*, by Mother Teresa, Edward Le Joly, and Jaya Chaliha (Element, 2000). **February 18:** John Lennon, "Man of the Decade" interview with Associated Television, December 2, 1969. Transcribed by www.beatlesinterviews.org from video copy of archived film footage. Available at http://www.beatlesinterviews.org/db1969.1202.beatles.html. **February 19:** John Keats, *The Complete Poetical Works and Letter of John Keats*, Cambridge Edition (Houghton Mifflin, 1899). **February 20:** Kemi Sogunle, *Beyond the Pain* (Kemi Sogunle, 2016). **February 21:** Rick Warren, "Remember: You're Not Home Yet," *Pastor Rick's Daily Hope* (August 8, 2016), pastorrick.com. **February 22:** Lord Byron, *Lord Byron Complete Works Ultimate Collection*, ed. Darryl Marks (Infinite Eternity Entertainment, 2013). **February 23:** John Owen, in *The Golden Treasury of Puritan Quotations*, ed. I. D. E. Thomas (Moody Press, 1975). **February 24:** John Keats, *The Complete Poetical Works and Letters of John Keats*, Cambridge Edition (Houghton Mifflin, 1899). **February 25:** David Ulrich, "Awakening Sight," *Parabola* Magazine 36, no. 3 (Fall 2011), 54–55. **February 26:** Pearl Cleage, *Some Things I Never Thought I'd Do* (One World, 2003), 214–215. **February 27:** Maria Erling and Mark Granquist, *The Augustana Story: Shaping Lutheran Identity in North America* (Augsburg Fortress, 2008), 129. **February 28:** Piper Kerman, *Orange Is the New Black: My Year in a Woman's Prison* (Spiegel & Grau, 2011), 278–279. **March 1:** Richard Rohr, *Everything Belongs: The Gift of Contemplative Prayer* (Crossroad, 2003), 46. **March 2:** Michael Harris, *The End of Absence: Reclaiming What We've Lost in a World of Constant Connection* (Current, 2014), 100. **March 3:** Kathleen S. Smith, *Stilling the Storm: Worship and Congregational Leadership in Difficult Times* (Alban Institute, 2006), 11. **March 4:** Liberty Hyde Bailey, *Country Life in America*, March 1903, 210. **March 5:** Matthew L. Skinner, "Preaching in a Time of Political Anxiety," *Working Preacher* (www.workingpreacher.org), March 14, 2017. **March 6:** Kobe Bryant, *Slam Online*, May 10, 2017. Available at http://www.slamonline.com/nba/kobe-bryant-isaiah-thomas-had-the-courage-to-ask-for-help/#GifvEgGQiOhBcdAj.97. **March 7:** Roger Housden, "Seeing the Good in Goodbyes," *Huffington Post* blog, November 2, 2011. Available at http://www.huffingtonpost.com/roger-housden/saying-goodbye_b_1068403.html. **March 8:** Martin Luther King Jr., *Strength to Love* (Fortress Press, 2010), gift ed., 48. **March 9:** Gail R. O'Day, "Jesus as Friend in the Gospel of John," *Interpretation* 58, no. 2 (April 2004), 144–157, 151. **March 10:** Corrie ten Boom, in T. J. McTavish, *A Theological Miscellany* (W Publishing Group, 2005), 116. **March 11:** Mary Oliver, "Sometimes," *Red Bird: Poems* (Beacon Press, 2009), 37. **March 12:** Marianne Williamson, *A Return to Love: Reflections on the Principles of "A Course in Miracles"* (HarperOne, 1996), 190. **March 13:** Brené Brown, "The Power of Vulnerability," TED Talk, June 2010, Houston, TX. **March 14:** Lauren Winner, *Wearing God* (HarperCollins, 2015). **March 15:** Bruce Reyes-Chow, *40 Days, 40 Prayers, 40 Words: Lenten Reflections* (Westminster John Knox, 2015), 2. **March 16:** Barbara Brown Taylor, *Leaving Church* (HarperOne, 2007), 107. **March 17:** Brian McLaren, *We Make the Road by Walking* (Jericho Books, 2015), xv. **March 18:** William Kent Krueger, *Ordinary Grace* (Atria Books, 2013), 270. **March 19:** Sara Miles, *Take This Bread* (Random House, 2007), 70. **March 20:** Martin Luther, *Luther's Works*, ed. Jaroslav Pelikan (Concordia, 1957), 22:520. **March 21:** Eugene Peterson, interview by Krista Tippet for *On Being* radio show and podcast, December 22, 2016. **March 22:** Wendell Berry, *The Gift of Good Land* (North Point Press, 1983), 272–281. **March 23:** Susan Palo Cherwien, "Christ, Burning Wisdom." From *O Blessed Spring*, copyright © 1997 Susan Palo Cherwien, admin. Augsburg Fortress. Reproduced by permission. **March 24:** Jean Janzen, based on Hildegard of Bingen, "O Holy Spirit, Root of Life," hymn 399, stanza 2. From *Evangelical Lutheran Worship*, copyright © 1991 Jean Janzen, admin. Augsburg Fortress. Reproduced by permission. **March 25:** Parker Palmer, *The Promise of Paradox* (John Wiley & Sons, 2008), 2. **March 26:** Maya Angelou, *Rainbow in the Cloud: The Wisdom and Spirit of Maya Angelou* (Random House, 2014). **March 27:** J. K. Rowling, *Harry Potter and the Deathly Hallows* (Scholastic, 2007), 328. **March 28:** Nicholas Wolterstorff, *Lament for a Son* (Eerdmans, 1987), 90. **March 29:** Anne Lamott, *Help, Thanks, Wow* (Riverhead Books, 2012), 16. **March 30:** Gail Ramshaw, *The Three-Day Feast* (Augsburg Fortress, 2004), 47–48. **March 31:** Thomas Lynch, *The Undertaking: Life Studies from the Dismal Trade* (Penguin Books, 1997), 191.